BIG IMPACT

A Goal-Setting Guide for Building Your Extraordinary Life

GOAL WHEEL INCLUDED

Lorin D. Beller

TABLE OF CONTENTS

INTRODUCTION

What is Big? Big is different for everyone. Big could be a lot of things—bigger house, more money, faster car, etc. Or Big could be a heart-focused, conscious-minded, bottom-line-driven entrepreneur/leader who cares deeply about their connections in the world, connections both personal and professional. Big could also mean caring about and being conscious of the impact we have each day. Big could be who we choose to surround ourselves with each day.

There are many ways to have impact in the world. **The biggest way we can have impact is just by being who we are right at this very moment (with no goals)!** Stay tuned for more on this in my next book! People with Big impact like to be conscious about who they are being in the present moment. This is critical to our impact in the world. Another way to set out to create positive impact is by setting goals.

Since 2002, many people have been using the goal-setting system that this book describes. And I am so proud of who they consciously choose to be each day and what they have accomplished over the years by using this goal-setting tool that you are about to learn about.

THE BIG PICTURE: CREATING YOUR VISION

"The greatest danger for most of us is not that our aim is too high and we miss it, but that it is too low and we reach it."
—Attributed to Michelangelo

Before we dive into creating goals, it is critical to know the direction we are going. The vision. So we will first create the vision.

The first step to creating the life that you want, no matter where you are at this very moment, is to have a vision. You might be unhappy in every aspect of your life—create a vision. You might be broke and behind in your bills—create a vision. You might be living a life that looks perfect from the outside and everyone around you thinks that you have it great, but inside you are miserable—create a vision.

What is a vision? It is creating a picture, written word, or image of the impact you know you can have in the world. A vision is a way you leave this world a better place than when you showed up in it. A vision is what you know deep down inside is possible for your life. Your vision is bigger than you are.

So many people are stuck in the past; they are looking out of the rearview mirror rather than the windshield. This is dangerous!

Having a vision gives you something to focus on each day rather than looking back to the past.

"Fix your eyes forward on what you can do, not back on what you cannot change."—Tom Clancy

---

So, how does one go about creating a vision? The process is quite simple.

First, take a few deep breaths (some of us might need more than a few!), become present, put your feet on the ground, and find this moment. After all, this is all we really have. What does it take for you to stop? Notice your surroundings. Notice the people around you. Who are they? How are they?

Notice your body. Notice how you feel inside. Notice your emotions. Notice your breathing. Slow down. What happens when we slow down? Some of us get sleepy, some go to sleep, some get excited, and some get distracted again from the moment. The only way to know and find your vision is by being present. Fully present.

Once you are able to be present, the next step is to notice what you are grateful for. Some of the things I'm grateful for include good health, relationships, a world that changes, access to delicious food, the conveniences of our time, a child's laugh, a hug from someone who cares, amazing and genuine leaders in our country, a kiss from a puppy, sparkles on the snow, sunshine on the water, friends that call at the perfect time, a thoughtful message from the perfect person; the list is endless. Stop and notice what you are grateful for. Actually, write it down; make a list. You might be amazed at how much there is to be grateful for. The best place to create a vision is from this place of gratitude.

Once we are present and in a state of gratitude, let's start with something that might seem odd or foreign. In your mind's eye, make yourself 20 years older than you are at this very moment. Imagine where you'd love for your life to be 20 years from today. If 20 years feels too far away, try 10 years. Let your body take you there. . . . Feel what it will be like 10 or 20 years from now.

Next, get out a piece of paper and begin to write about this image that you see. Writing does one of two things. It allows us to capture something we want to savor or let go of something we want to rid ourselves of, depending on the intention we have for writing. Whatever the intention, writing gets it out of our heads. In our head is not where we want to keep things.

We want to keep our mind free to work, free from clutter, and free from emotion. We want to keep it nimble and in good form, which allows us to use both sides of the brain more readily. We keep way too much in there. Think of your brain as being like a suitcase with two big compartments (left and right brain).

By clearing the clutter, we allow both sides to function as they were intended.

The right side of the brain is creative, soulful, empathetic, and magical—the savior. The left side of the brain is analytical, practical, and critical—the saboteur. We need both. In business, many of us use much more of our left brain, but we are entering a new age. Daniel Pink discusses it in his book, *A Whole New Mind: Why Right-Brainers Will Rule the Future*. Business in this new age is going to begin to thrive as we become much more creative, much more into free thinking and more intention focused rather than goal focused. By freeing our brains from the details of life through writing things down, our brains become more relaxed. We are, therefore, able to be more creative and our ability to think outside the box is increased. This "outside the box" way of approaching business actually allows for more wild success.

So relax, breathe, and become present. Notice all that you have to be grateful for, and when that list is exhausted, begin to write your vision story.

Remember that a vision story is just that: a story. It is all made up! But it is your vision of what you know deep inside is possible for your life. It is what you know you were put on this planet to do and how you can and will have influence. This story is not "how" you will do it, it is "where you are" and where the world is when you implement and use your life to influence the world. It is a snapshot of where you will be after 10 or 20 years of working and living in your most magical and impactful place.

Get out a piece of paper, or better yet, open a blank journal. While reading this chapter, when you feel or begin to get a sense of your life 10 or 20 years from now, start writing.

Here are some questions that might help your writing to flow. Choose 10 or 20 years, according to where you are in your life at present.

10 or 20 years from now:

- Where do you live?

- What is your home/space like?

- What is the temperature where you are?

- Where have you traveled?

- Where is your family?

- How are they?

- What is your mood?

- How do you spend your time?

- What kinds of foods are you eating?

- What makes you laugh?

- What is the tone of the day?

- What is the pace of the day?

- What are the smells in the air?

- Who is around you?

- What is the world like now?

- What is the impact you have had on the world?

- How does that segment of the world see you?

- What is different about you now?

- What types of sounds are around you?

- What do you see around you?

Add in any details that energize you. Let your mind be creative.

Have fun with this exercise. Try to limit the vision to one page.

There are many reasons to have a vision. Everyone who completes this exercise thinks that it is for tomorrow, but it is truly an exercise that services us today. We will spend much more time on this in the following chapters. To reiterate, because it is a critical point, creating a vision is not for tomorrow; it is to help inform us today.

As the process unfolds throughout this book, this statement will become more and more clear. The founder of one of our most successful Internet-based companies says it quite succinctly:

"If you think about the long term, then you can really make good life decisions that you won't regret later."—Jeff Bezos, founder of Amazon.com

---

Remember that creating a vision for your life and your impact in the world is not set in stone. This vision document is meant to be changed, updated, and tweaked on a regular basis. It will change. It will evolve. It will morph. This quote by a famous musician says it best:

"Map out your future, but do it in pencil."—Jon Bon Jovi

When people write their vision, they often find themselves thinking, "How will I ever do this?" The how is not important at the moment; we'll get to the how later. Rather, we want your vision to be so empowering, so inspiring, that you are excited to get started! When you write that vision, you listen more with the right side of your brain, not the left side that is always questioning if you can really accomplish anything.

The same thing has been said in the words of another:

"When I dare to be powerful, to use my strength in the service of my vision, then it becomes less and less important whether I am afraid."—Audre Lorde

So many times we see ourselves as victims or waste our time being angry, but when we have a vision, we step out of that unproductive mode and become our best selves. We become less hung up on the issues in our life and refocus on our vision, which has us more constantly in our best self.

"People who consider themselves victims of their circumstances will always remain victims unless they develop a greater vision for their lives."—Stedman Graham

One of the best books I've ever read is *Man's Search for Meaning* by Viktor E. Frankl. Having a vision helps us find meaning in life—in our lives and the lives of others. It helps us hold the world more sacred. When we have a vision, we begin to see life as a resource to be taken care of rather than taken for granted.

"One must care about a world one will not see."
—Bertrand Russell

The other reason for a vision for our lives is that without one, we tend to wander all over the world. That is not to say this a bad thing. Wandering has its place in the journey, for sure. We find new and amazing things while wandering. But when we feel deep inside that there is something that is our job to do on this planet, and we identify it by writing it down, we tend to make decisions that keep us on a particular path, which more quickly takes us to our vision.

"If you don't know where you are going, you might wind up someplace else."—Yogi Berra

Another thing about vision is that it is not about reaching it!

It is about moving toward it each day. Sometimes we miss it and sometimes we go way beyond it, but where would we be without the aim?

"Aim for the moon. Even if you miss, you'll land among the stars."—Unknown

COMMITMENT

There is another very important part of a vision that we have not yet discussed. It is commitment. Having a vision without a commitment to it virtually makes it null and void. It is just a possibility. Once a commitment has been made, something within us shifts. There are no options. Yes, there are various ways of reaching it, but the end goal, the end vision, is in stone. The essence of the vision has been written in indelible ink. This is an important ingredient when writing your vision. The details of the vision may change and vary, but its essence does not. The feeling of it does not change.

Commitment also gives us faith in the story and, more importantly, faith in ourselves. This ingredient tends not to be spoken of when it comes to creating and manifesting goals, but leaving it out would be a destructive mistake in the process. As you create and write your vision, be sure that it is something you are committed to, no matter what! There is no timeline in a vision.

There are no "hows" in a vision. It is just the end image that you are committing to and having faith in.

"The secret of making something work in your lives is, first of all, the deep desire to make it work; then the faith [commitment] and belief that it can work; then to hold that clear definite vision in your consciousness and see it working out step by step, without one thought of doubt or disbelief."— Eileen Caddy

Commitment is a critical ingredient in reaching your goals. Robert Conklin, teacher, author, and speaker, says it well, "If you make the unconditional commitment to reach your most important goals, if the strength of your decision is sufficient, you will find the way and the power to achieve your goals."

Too many times I see people who have a goal but have no commitment, and this makes for lousy motivation to complete it. Many successful people will say, "There was not an option." They made the decision to accomplish the goal. There were no excuses. Nothing got in the way, or if it did, it was seen as a temporary hurdle to overcome, nothing more.

W. E. B. DuBois (1868–1963), civil rights activist and author, says it best, "There is in this world no such force as the force of a man determined to rise." The key word here is *determined*. When we are determined to reach a certain goal or accomplishment, nothing gets in our way for long. There is an energy that comes with that person that is unstoppable. You can tell by how they walk, how they talk, and how they carry themselves.

As you create your vision, be sure you are writing about what you want, not what you do not want. This puts energy on the appropriate aspects of what you want to create. For example, if you want to "create more joy and peace in the world," say that, rather than saying you want to "stop focusing on the bad things that are happening in the world." Your words matter. Choose them thoughtfully. If you are truly writing your own genuine vision (not your mother's, not your father's, not your spouse's, not your kids'—yours!), you will find this process enlightening, freeing, inspiring, energizing, and motivating. If you keep it fresh and read it often, it will continue to have an impact on your day—as long as you are making choices and taking daily action that moves you toward that vision.

"The moment of enlightenment is when a person's dreams of possibilities become images of probabilities."—Vic Braden

As you approach this exercise, always start with the end in mind: the vision that you want to reach. Do not start with the messy desk or the long to-do list that has you on a hamster wheel each day. If you start here, you will get more of the same.

If you start at the end, you may find that some of that stuff on the desk might really belong in the trash!

Next, you need to have faith in yourself to make the goal happen. You need to have faith in the world around you that the perfect things will come at the perfect time to manifest the goals. Be open to the flow. Sometimes we want things in a certain time frame, but they come much sooner or much later. Notice what you are attracting. This is a great clue as to what you are putting energy into. It also gives you feedback as to where to next focus your energy.

Big Impact

THE PIECES AND THE PARTS

Goals are meant to be aimed at. Sometimes we work very hard to accomplish them. Other times we work really hard and we end up not accomplishing them. But what matters is that our heart is into the goal, in the moment. We have to want the goal. Not begrudgingly go after it, or even gently go after it, but wildly go after it. We must move toward it—that is the purpose of a goal. And what is even more important than the goal is *who we become while on our journey toward a goal.*

As humans, I believe we were born to strive to be our best, and that we have the desire to have a positive impact on the world. So it is in our basic instincts to have dreams, desires, wants, and needs. If we listen to our intuition, there are tremendous goals that are waiting to be noticed, captured, and strived for. It is our job to listen to our inner desires.

First, I will define some important words in the goal-setting process.

INTENTION

What is an intention?

Intention is as Merriam-Webster defines it: "The thing that you plan to do or achieve; an aim or purpose." And it goes on to say it's "a determination to act in a certain way."

I like to think about intentions as how we will *be* (or act) as we move toward something we want to accomplish. Intention matters! Intention is the energy with which we go about something. If we go about something begrudgingly, we generally find that we have a shabby end result, if we even reach the end. And if we go about something with presence and excitement, we have a vastly different result in the end most of the time. How we go about something, anything, matters. This quote says it best:

"Each decision we make, each action we take, is born out of an intention."—Sharon Salzberg

---

INTUITION

What is our intuition?

Intuition is that small voice (sometimes not so small) that speaks to us often about what we should or should not do. With practice, we get better and better at listening to it.

Merriam-Webster defines intuition as "a natural ability or power that makes it possible to know something without any proof or evidence; a feeling that guides a person to act a certain way without fully understanding why."

I believe that intuition is a big part of the goal-setting process. Sometimes when it is time to set a fresh set of goals (which is anytime we feel the need to regroup, not just at the beginning of a new year. It is when we want or need to be inspired and create a fresh perspective for ourselves!), we need to listen to our intuition regarding what is next for us. What is calling us?

I love the Mary Oliver quote: "Tell me, what is it you plan to do with your one wild and precious life?"

When we ask ourselves that question, then sit quietly and listen, we hear intuition speaking to us, calling to us to move toward some new, powerful, fun goals.

GOAL

What is a goal?

Merriam-Webster defines a goal as something that you are trying to do or achieve.

There are many, many types of goals. In our Entrepreneurial Development program, we focus on two different types of goals:

The first is a **Bold Action or a Measurable Goal (BA).** These are both *big goals*. This type of goal is very specific and has a very clear ending with the ability to check it off as complete. For example, losing 20 pounds, writing a book, going someplace you've always wanted to go, saving a certain amount of money, running a marathon, going to a full-day meditation class, etc. It is easy to see when these goals get set, planned, worked at, and then completed. We can check them off as bucket-list kinds of accomplishments.

The other type of goal is what we call **Daily or Weekly Habit Goals (DH).** These types of goals are more lifestyle goals. By doing them regularly, we truly change the fabric of our life. Some examples of these would be reading 30 minutes per day, walking every morning, meditating 20 minutes per day, drinking eight glasses of water per day, meeting with your team (business) weekly, spending quality time with your child daily, stretching for 15 minutes every day, making one outreach call per day to grow the business, etc. You can see that by doing such things regularly we change our lives. We change our business, we change our family, we change our health—we change.

Both of these types of goals are critical to our success and our achievement. A lot of times it takes *daily habits* to accomplish *big goals*. (And that is why we hire coaches—in order to have accountability along the way.)

A goal is defined by dictionary.com as "the end toward which effort is directed."

Goals need to be:

- Specific

- Measurable, and

- Time-targeted

For example:

- I will exercise 10 minutes per day (DH).

- I will acknowledge my partner positively three times per day (DH).

- I will complete writing content for my book by April 30th (BA).

- I will attend a women's retreat for me by September (BA).

- I will buy a new "green car" next year (BA).

- I will increase my income by 25% by the end of this year (BA).

- I will work on being my best self 90% of the time, one week at a time, rating myself at the end of each week this year (DH).

- I will enroll my daughter in swim classes this summer (BA).

- I will spend 30 minutes of quality time with my daughter each day (DH).

- I will hike one Adirondack mountain with friends this year (BA).

- I will speak with five new potential clients each week this year and keep track of each relationship in my new customer relationship management tool (DH).

- I will speak publicly to audiences larger than 100 at least 20 times this year (DH).

As you can see by the example list above, some goals are forever ongoing. In other words, we are trying to create a new lifestyle or business routine. We call these daily habits. Other goals are one-time goals that we can complete and check off. Both are goals and are very different. We need both kinds of goals to make significant changes in our lives and businesses.

It does not matter what area your goals fall into; what matters most is that they get written down.

Writing down your goals can be accomplished in any number of ways. Just begin by writing them down in a blank journal or on a piece of paper, adding magazine photos or recording them in whatever way is most fun for you. The key here, as you think of goals you want to achieve, is to capture them in any format that speaks to you.

Marc Allen, the author of *The Greatest Secret of All: Moving Beyond Abundance to a Life of True Fulfillment*, says it well, "The simple step of writing down your ideal scene can lead you to discover the unfailing natural laws of manifestation."

In the January 2009 issue of *Real Simple*, it was reported that 72% of women say happiness lies in making progress toward their goals, even if they never achieve them! Having a vision with a plan creates more joy. I have witnessed this hundreds of times. I believe the reason this is true is that we begin working toward things that are bigger than ourselves.

It gets our egos out of the way. We think less about ourselves and more about the impact we want to have, and how to help others.

The other thing that I have witnessed is that if this process is created out of pure joy and is aligned with the vision, the Universe begins to work with us. (Feel free to use your own word here: God, Creator, the World, etc.) I like to think of it as a process of "co-creation." We do not do it by ourselves and the Universe does not do it by itself; we co-create it. Putting goals and visions on paper helps the world around us know what we want. It is a form of "asking." David S. Jordan, the most influential of all American ichthyologists, said: "The world steps aside to let any man pass if he knows where he is going." But first, it is our responsibility as a human on this planet to know where we are going.

When we hear stories of people who are wildly successful in setting and obtaining goals, we often say, "They had it easy," or "Life just went their way." But they did their part. They knew where they were going. Knowing is a key ingredient.

We tend to ignore the knowing inside of us. This is one of the important keys to success—listening to that knowing and taking action based on that knowing.

Once our goals are written down, it is critical to notice where we put our energy, what we focus on, and what we keep in our mind's eye.

Some people have their annual goals with them at all times and look at the goals every day! This is a perfect example of the choice we have about where we put our energy.

You can choose to focus attention consistently on your goals. The result is that your thoughts and actions are consistently aligned with your goals. This is a unique skill that creates success!

Kathleen Norris (1880–1966), an American novelist who was the highest-paid female writer of her time, said, "Before you begin a thing, remind yourself that difficulties and delays quite impossible to foresee are ahead. You can only see one thing clearly, and that is your goal. Form a mental vision of that and cling to it through thick and thin."

Big Impact

CATEGORIES OF GOALS

Goals fall into many different categories. We start with the following eight areas of our lives: personal or spiritual growth, health, business or career, money, our significant relationship (spouse/partner), family and friends, fun and recreation, and finally, environment. I want to outline these areas so that you start to see how important it is to look at all of them.

PERSONAL OR SPIRITUAL GROWTH

This area is about our own personal growth: things that you want to learn or experience personally. It also can be about your spiritual growth. By that I do not mean religious, unless you have personal goals in that aspect of your life. The best way to outline this particular area is by sharing some popular examples. However, these are just a few ideas; anything you personally want to do is really what goes in this area. Some examples are:

- To learn to speak French
- To learn to meditate
- To take a creative writing class
- To learn to cook vegetarian
- To spend more time alone and nurture myself
- To learn to ballroom dance
- To take singing lessons
- To read 12 books
- To keep a daily gratitude journal
- To join and attend a book club

Just to name a few!

HEALTH

This is an area in which we all seem to easily set goals when it is a new year. We say things to ourselves like: "This is the year that I am going to lose 20 pounds. I am going to cut back on drinking wine. I am going to start going to the gym," etc. These are just a few that I hear often. But I define health a bit more broadly than most. I like to think about it in relation to our mind, our body, and our spirit (energy).

Our **mind health** is what keeps our thoughts calm, upbeat, positive, and the "I" of who we are—in charge of our thoughts rather than our thoughts running us (this can get very deep and cross over into the area of personal or spiritual growth). But it is mind health that has us get very aware and conscious of our thoughts so that we are in charge of them. My Buddhist friends call it "taming the monkeys" (of our mind). When we speak with successful people, if we listen, we will see that they are very much in charge of their thoughts. And they work at that probably more than anything else. It is truly a practice. Some examples of goals in this area would be:

Meditating daily
Walking in silence daily (walking meditation)
Choosing gratitude when frustrated
Taking time four times per day to get present and notice
Taking time to journal daily regarding this moment
Just to name a few!

Our **body health** is our physical body, internally and externally. This would include what we eat (or do not eat) as well as our exercise and every aspect of our physical health. This is the area that we focus on in the Western world: what our bodies look like. Some goals in this area might be:

- Getting to 120 pounds
- Going to the gym three times per week
- Walking daily
- Riding my bike three times per week
- Doing yoga 15 minutes per day

It also could be:
- Cutting out sugar
- Becoming a vegetarian
- Going gluten free
- Eating more fruits and vegetables
- Drinking eight glasses of water per day
- Noticing and being conscious of our daily energy

Just to name a few!

Our **spirit or energy health** is the demeanor or energy with which we go about life every day. Some people have energy that is attracting, and they are sort of like a magnet—we want to be around them. They are fun, upbeat, and it generally seems that life is easy for them. But the truth is, they have healthy energy in that moment and they work to be there as much of the time as possible. Our energy matters. I believe that like mind health (we choose to practice how we think), we also choose to create our energy. Some people can be negative, or constantly gossiping, or have a bullying tone, and we react by having a heavy or tired energy after being around them. Energy health can directly affect our level of success, and when I use the word *success,* I do not mean strictly money (more on this later). Energy health is a choice when we begin to set goals around this area. Some examples of goals around our energy health might be:

Practice Qigong three times per week. According to the National Qigong Association's website, "Qigong is an ancient Chinese health care system that integrates physical postures, breathing techniques and focused intention. The word Qigong (Chi Kung) is made up of two Chinese words. Qi is pronounced *chee* and is usually translated to mean the life force or vital energy that flows through all things in the universe. The second word, Gong, pronounced *gung*, means accomplishment, or skill that is cultivated through steady practice. Together, Qigong (Chi Kung) means cultivating energy. It is a system practiced for health maintenance, healing and increasing vitality."

Go to an acupuncturist monthly. Acupuncturists are trained to use needles to work with our body's energy.

Get shiatsu monthly. Shiatsu is a form of acupressure that originated in Japan.

Just to name a few!

The above are all forms of "adjusting our energy" where others are assisting in manipulating our energy for us. But below are some ways that we can practice being more in charge of our own energy:

- Get sufficient sleep each night
- Breathe and pause regularly
- Learn to develop healthy boundaries
- Develop a self-care routine
- Raise your awareness about your own energy
- Keep an energy journal
- Read a book on the topic
- Practice staying in the present moment

Just to name a few!

As you can see, there are so many ways to take care of ourselves. And by thinking about our health with a three-pronged approach, we will deepen our overall health and well-being. The three areas are interrelated, and as we work on all three we become exponentially better at all of them, but it first takes being aware that health has many facets.

BUSINESS OR CAREER

I use this section for anything related to business or career. If you are a student, it may be your schoolwork. If you are a stay-at-home mom, it may be volunteer work that you want to do or taking care of the household. If you are an entrepreneur, it is your business. If you have a job and work for someone—this is the area. I believe that we all have a type of work. This is the place that your "work desires" get identified. It is *not* about making money. . . . But often it is the way we make money. So let's break it up.

If you are a student (of any age), your goals might be:
- To study X hours every night
- To take X number of courses per semester
- To study under someone that you want to learn from
- To get a certain grade (but I prefer to focus on the process of learning rather than the grade)

Just to name a few!

If you are a stay-at-home mom, your goals might be:
- To be home for the kids when they get home.
- To volunteer in each of your children's classrooms.
- To help each of your children to find a volunteer organization to be a part of.
- To not do housework when the kids are home so that you get to spend quality time with them.

Just to name a few!

If you have your own business, your goals might be:
- To write an e-book
- To launch a new product
- To find three new referral partners
- To hire an assistant
- To go to an industry conference

Just to name a few!

If you are working at a job, your goals might be:
- To have weekly meetings with your team
- To work more closely with a certain department
- To work on your communication skills
- To attend a conference specifically for your role

Just to name a few!

MONEY

This is where we identify anything to do with money. And it is about *you*. What you might want to earn, what you might want to save, what you might want to give away, or your contribution to the world from your earnings. If you have all of that handled, perhaps it is passing on those four aspects of money (saving, spending, making, and donating) to your children. Another great way to use this particular area is to notice your relationship with money. If you are someone who struggles with earning "enough" or feeling that you never have enough, then some goals around your *relationship with money* might be in order in this area. It is also very helpful to have a goal to work within a monthly, weekly, or annual budget if you find yourself in debt too often. If you have more debt than you would like, then another goal might be to pay off debt. There are many ways to think about your money goals. Just to name a few!

To be clear, this is not just about *getting* more money but about what **you can do to develop yourself** and your skills to improve your relationship with money.

SIGNIFICANT OTHER

If you are currently in a relationship, then this is the place for your relationship goals. However, this is *not* the place for your goals for the other person! We are only in charge of ourselves in the relationship. So think about *your* goals in the relationship. For example, if you want to have a more intimate relationship with your partner, I would highly recommend looking at *your part* in how *you* can create more intimacy rather than putting a goal down for the other person, hoping they will go along with it.

One of my favorite examples of a goal here is from one of the clients that I have worked with for over a decade. He has a goal every year to touch his wife every time she is within arm's length. He feels that it is one of the key ingredients to his 25+ years of happy marriage.

A great book that might help here is *The 5 Love Languages*, by Gary Chapman. I love this book because it helps us know what our partner's love language is and then speak (do) more of that, rather than more of what we think she or he wants. The five love languages are:

- Physical touch
- Quality time together
- Acts of service
- Receiving gifts, and
- Words of affirmation

You can find the test online (www.5lovelanguages.com) and you can both take it. Then you can design *your* goals for the relationship. This is just a suggestion and one that will help you do things for developing the relationship. But remember, again, these are *your* goals that *you* are responsible for, not the other person. You can also take this test for or with your children so that you are better able to understand each child's love language. They are different!

Some other goals that you might want to ponder would be:

- To be more curious about your partner, ask more questions (quality time)
- Make eye contact when you have a conversation for 10 minutes each day (quality time)
- You being responsible for reaching out and touching lovingly (physical touch) on a regular basis
- If your partner is the one who is always responsible for dinner, for you to take on that chore one day per week (act of service)
- Every time you travel, to bring home a little gift (receiving gifts)
- At the end of each day, acknowledge your partner for something you appreciate (words of affirmation)

Just to name a few!

If you are not in a significant relationship, this is the place to have goals if you want to be in a relationship. For example, you may have a goal of getting involved in some group where you can meet new people, or meeting one new person per week, or going out weekly just to meet people, etc.

If you are not in a relationship and actually don't care to be, identify how and what you want to do to take care of yourself above and beyond your health. After all, it is our relationship with ourselves that is the most important. In that healthy relationship, all other healthy and fulfilling relationships are possible.

FAMILY AND FRIENDS

Some people feel that your family members are your friends and your friends are your family. If you feel that way, then this portion of your life, like significant other, is "your part" of what you want to accomplish in this area. For example, it may be to connect weekly by making a phone call, or seeing them monthly. Another might be to be more curious about them and how they are. It may be to listen more. If you need or want to think about these two groups of people differently, that's fine. Some people do not see their family as friends and their friends as family. Either way, it is important to be clear on what your goals are for yourself with these groups of people.

For years I developed amazing close friendships. I think of my friends as my family and my family as my friends. And when I went through a very challenging time in my life, I leaned on them quite a bit, more than I ever had. I was so grateful for such strong and supportive relationships during that time. Afterward, I had to get clear that it was time to give back, and my goals reflected that for a few years. Just to be clear, this is the area where you think about what you want to do to be responsible for building these relationships. It is about your behavior, not theirs.

Some examples of goals in this area might be:
- Spend quality time with your children daily
- Reach out to three friends per week to check in with them and see how they are
- Take an elderly parent or friend out to lunch weekly

Just to name a few!

FUN AND RECREATION

This area has two important things to think about. The first is how and what you want to do to bring more fun, adventure, and aliveness to all aspects of your life. In other words, to "live out loud" more!

The other part is to think about the fun things that you want to do.

The former is more of a way of being in all parts of your life and the latter is more of reaching goals that you have for yourself. I purposely split this particular area in this way because I constantly hear people saying things like, "I want more fun in my life," or "I want more adventure in my life," or "I want more excitement," and when I hear this, I know it is not just about scheduling a vacation this year—that will not fulfill that need to "live out loud" more.

What's needed is a fresh zest for life, and that takes approaching your whole life with more of an intention overall. When you begin to think about your life as more of an adventure, we change the entire "feeling" of life, and that *is* possible. So think about this area in both ways, not just for one week of the year.

And I want to caution you, I find so many people saying that they will be happy when they have that new car, or house, or job, or relationship, or something. And what I know is, that is a lie you are telling yourself. If we really think that the new house or new car will make us happy, we are setting ourselves up for a big ol' failure. After the newness of that shiny new object wears off, we go back to the same old level of happiness again. I would not encourage you to go after these things for happiness but to instead find happiness right where you are, *and* go after that new car if you really want it, but know that it is not the car that creates an extraordinary life—it is how we engage with life that creates an extraordinary life.

Some goals here might be:
- Bring fun to all that I do
- Lighten up rather than take it all so seriously
- Find the learning from mistakes and celebrate that learning
- In the absurd, find the humor—practice this regularly

Just to name a few!

And some typical goals I see in this area are:
- Travel to _____ (you fill in the blank)
- Throw a party for _____
- Go on a hot air balloon ride (with friends I will invite, or go alone if no one else wants to go)
- Or any other fun thing that you've always wanted to do

Just to name a few!

ENVIRONMENT

Our environment is literally where we live. It is our home, our car, our local community, and our virtual community. It is our world in the respect that you think about it. So you get to decide how you want to impact your environment. I like to think about how I want my environment to *feel* and look when I am in it. From there I can decide how I want to change it.

I have seen some really creative goals in this area over the years.

Some have been:
- Declutter every room of my house
- Clean up trash every six months around my neighborhood streets with my kids
- Grow a garden
- Play peaceful music every day in my home

- Light a candle every day in my home
- Hire a housecleaner this year
- Move to _____
- Buy a home in X neighborhood
- Buy a new car

Just to name a few!

THE GOAL WHEEL

So now let's put all of this together in our one-page goal-setting tool. Go to http://www.lorinbeller.com/download-your-2018-goal-wheel-here/ to find your own downloadable copy of the goal wheel.

Let's identify all the pieces or parts of the goal wheel:

The **inner circle** contains all the *intentions* or ways you want to be as you go about your goals for the year. The easiest way to think about it is that in order to accomplish this goal, I want to *be* _____.
You can have an intention for all areas of your life!

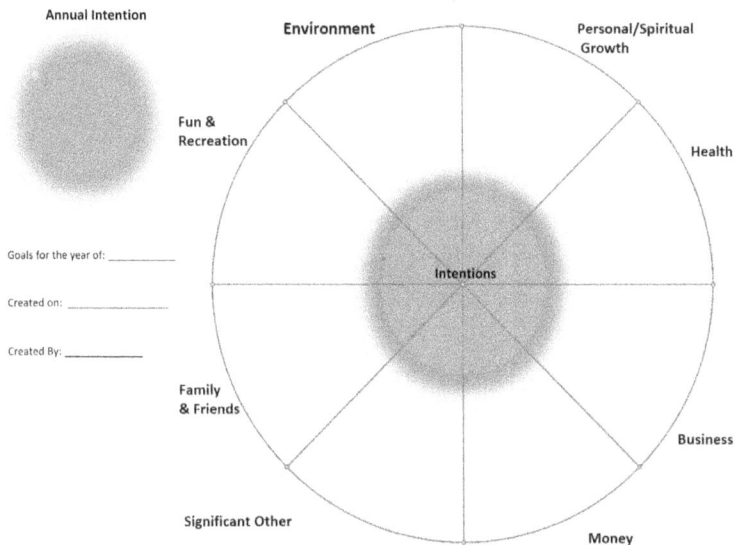

Annual Intention

Goals for the year of: _____

Created on: _____

Created By: _____

Environment

Personal/Spiritual Growth

Fun & Recreation

Health

Intentions

Family & Friends

Business

Significant Other

Money

Intentions are either one word or a short phrase. I like to think of them as being like bookends to our goals. My favorite example is the intention that I use in the area of health. I have a few goals this year:

- To drink 60–72 ounces of water every day
- To stretch every day (yoga 15 minutes)
- To meditate or do a present-moment exercise each day
- Do plank for one minute each day

Now in my mind, if I do those things daily (in addition to what I am already doing), I will *be buff!* And I like that! Buff to me is sexy, it is strong, it is in charge of me! I want that! And only I can create that. So that motivates me to work on implementing my new daily routine. It is up to me to be fully responsible for my actions in order to create that. *Responsibility.* And if I do implement it over the course of the year, do you think I will *be buff?!* So the intentions motivate. They are also the end game, but most importantly they get me stepping into *buff* each day—*today.* I choose to get conscious about that. Intentions are powerful. So my health intention is: Be buff.

Some people have a good sense of their goals, so they write their goals first and see what the intention needs to be to accomplish those goals. Other people know the intention first and then fill in the goals because they have a sense of the new energy they are going for in that part of their life.

I want to point out something extremely important here: these ways of being are authentic. You are not being fake; you are consciously being someone you want to be. There is zero manipulation. There is zero motive. There is zero fakeness. Instead you are consciously trying to be your best self for your own self. This is consciously who you know you are at your core. And there is a tremendous ripple effect when we step into our genuine and authentic best selves for only good intent.

The *goals* that you have go in the **white outer portion of the circle**. These need to be either bold action/measurable goals, such as:

I will write and publish the book by June.
Or
I will save $12,000 by December.
Or
I will invite my friends to do a hot air balloon ride by July.

These are measurable, bold actions that we can check off as *done*!

Or you might be writing new habits that would look more like this:

I will drink eight glasses of water every day starting January 1.
Or
I will write every morning for 20 minutes before heading out the door.
Or
I will take Mom to lunch every Wednesday.
Or
I will volunteer with my daughter every Saturday.

These are examples of new daily or weekly habits that you want to accomplish.

Taking the time to write all your goals down is life changing. Written goals have more power because of the clarity in how you see them when you take the time to get the goals out of your head and onto paper. Thoughts are energy, words are energy, and the written word is energy. In my first book we talk about the Big Fish Principles, and the first principle is: Give energy to that which you want to grow.

Some people worry about which goals go where, but what is most important is that you capture the goals and write them in the wheel.

ANNUAL INTENTION

The annual intention is the *smaller bubble in the top left* of the one-page goal wheel. This annual intention is your overarching *intention* for the year . . . sort of your North Star in how you want to focus your energy overall. When you hit a challenge, that intention will be what guides you forward through the challenge. This can be a game changer of a tool!

Your annual intention gives you a focus for the year, a focus for an overall way of being that transforms you. Therefore, there are nine intentions, one for each of the eight areas plus one for the year.

For example, let's say that you want to create your life to be more radiant. In other words, you want to be your brightest light possible in the world as you walk around in it. You know that in that place you connect well with people wherever you go. So you set your annual intention as RADIANT SPIRIT.

Another one of my favorite annual intentions that I have seen used by someone was GIVE LOVE TO THIS. So whatever you are doing, experiencing, interacting with, your annual intention is to give love to this. Powerful. Game changer of a focus.

THE POWER OF INTENTION WITH GOALS

Many people wonder why we need both goals and intentions. Years ago, I used to believe that goals were more important than intentions, but after doing this for 15+ years, I am becoming convinced that the intention is actually more important. When we live from the intention, the goals show up and we stay more true to ourselves. ***The real power is in the combination of the two.***

Intention has been defined as "the state of a person's mind that directs his or her actions toward a specific object," or "a determination to act in a certain way."

For the purpose of helping set and achieve goals, I like to think of intention as a way of being in order to reach a goal. For example, if we are trying to reach our highest income yet, are we doing it with joy and vigor or stress and frustration? We all know that doing anything with more stress and frustration is nowhere near as much fun. It will take longer and make the process harder. If we approach the goal with joy, vigor, positive energy, and excitement, we naturally attract people to join us in the process. Intention matters. And, if we are more conscious of our intentions and our "way of being" to create our goals, we tend to do more great work, too!

Your intentions should speak to you and help you in a way that guides you in how to be in that particular area of your life or work in order to create your goals. When we stay in that place and work on our goals, they are more apt to happen with ease. We all know people who set out to accomplish something big and make it look easy. It looks like no effort was expended; they say it, and it happens like magic. It is all about their intent. Intent makes life easier and makes life fun.

As part of a women's retreat, I did the fire walk, where I literally walked on hot coals, yet I did not burn my feet—not one tiny blister. This was because of the state in which I walked through the fire. My state of mind was one that was high energy, with the intention only to walk and be safe, healthy, and powerful. If I had worried about getting burned and looked down at the coals with fear, my intention would have been very different. My energy and intent were very conscious, causing successful results.

Intentions take us to the root of how we want to be as we work on this area of our life.

We go into meetings for the sake of having a meeting. We travel to places because someone asked us to, but seldom do we ask, "What is our group intention, and what is our own intention for this meeting, conversation, or get-together?"

Having an intention for the things we do changes everything.

Remember that intention is defined as "the goal or purpose behind a specific action or set of actions."

Creating intention does a few things:

- Creates efficiency

- Creates direction

- Creates leadership

- Creates a natural agenda

- Creates awareness

It also creates a time for doing or a time for being, but it is clear either way.

As a business tool, thinking about our intention for all that we are doing changes everything. I was recently speaking with a client who called a meeting with the owners of a competitor company because they were interested in purchasing her company. She had given them lots of information about her company, including its financials and structure. Her intuition was telling her that they needed to sit down and talk, and she listened to that intuition. She called the meeting, but as the meeting date grew near, she became concerned. After exploring what her specific concerns were, we realized that while she used her intuition and asked for the meeting, she was stressed over it. She did not have an intention for the meeting, and she was worried about the direction it could take. After we discussed what she wanted her intention to be, immediately an agenda was created. Once she realized she was actually in charge of the meeting, her confidence returned.

Another great use of intention comes into play when we are writing. As business owners, we journal, we write out goals, and we write business plans, but our intention for writing varies. For example, we might write journal entries about places we have been to savor the memories. We might journal about our challenges, in order to work through them. We might journal just to give ourselves space to be creative about our ideas. When it comes to utilizing writing as a business skill, intention is a critical ingredient.

Setting intentions as well as goals is extremely powerful. In our Entrepreneurial Development program, we have been doing this for years. For example, if in business we have a number of goals but our overall intention is to be known as the expert within a certain niche market, our goals will take us to that place. Having that intention will also tend to motivate us to be consistent in working on our goals, so the intention can do two things:

1) It can help us be the expert now.

2) It can motivate us to get to that end place.

The intention is an extremely powerful part of the goal-setting process. Turn back to the goal wheel included in Chapter 4 (p. 35). You will see in the diagram that there is a section labeled "Intention" for each of the eight goal-setting areas. Here are some examples of intentions for various parts of our lives:

Health: To be buff

Career/Business: To be the expert in my niche

Money: To feel abundance

Significant Other: To be compassionate

Family/Friends: Connection

Recreation: Free to play

Environment: To be green

Personal/Spiritual Growth: To honor all

These are just some examples of intentions. They can be seen as goals as well, but the difference is that they are all ways of being rather than things we can do and cross off the list. As we become conscious of how we want to be, our actions tend to change and we become more bold and consistent. They also have more meaning because there is a deeper intention behind actions that we are conscious of.

I believe that it is critical for us to have an intention set prior to going into a meeting. Sometimes it makes sense to share the intention; sometimes it does not. Remember the client that we discussed earlier? When she clarified her intention for setting the meeting in the first place, the agenda fell right into place.

We can also have intentions when it comes to family. I have an intention each day when I pick up my daughter from school to connect with her to find out about her day. Each time I pick her up, my intention is to connect. I do not tell her that, but I am sure she gets a sense of that each day. I do not make or receive phone calls on our ride home. I do not listen to the radio. I only drive and interact with her. I ask her about her day and share a bit about mine. It is only a twenty-five-minute ride each way, but it is a time that I have carved out as sacred time to connect only with my daughter.

What I have noticed is that if we have preset intentions for relationships, we tend to reach the goal much more quickly and efficiently because there is nothing distracting us from that intention. Multitasking when we have an intention only delays the result and sometimes actually inhibits the intention! Single-mindedness is critical.

Another family-specific example that may be helpful is the following: Let's say that we have two families and both have different intentions each night at dinner. One family's intention is connection with each other. The other family's intention is to eat.

Neither intention is good or bad, but each intention will create a very different experience. The family with the intention of connection will most likely be having meaningful conversation. They will be listening to each other's words. They will be asking curious questions like, "What did you do today?" "Did you enjoy it?" "Sounds like it was a challenge; how did you handle it?" While they are talking and sharing with each other, they will be eating the food in front of them, but most likely they will not discuss in detail the food, the weather, what is on TV, or be gossiping about someone else who is not at the table. The focus will be on each other.

On the other hand, the other family will be focusing strictly on the food and consuming it. There may not be much interaction with each other. They might discuss some basic topic of conversation to be polite while eating, but the conversation will be light and will not be focused on connecting. But, hey, they will have gotten the job done; plates will be clean!

If we observe the two families without being able to hear the conversation, they might not look too different, but the outcome would be drastically different. So we can have intentions for all aspects of our lives. This process raises consciousness.

Intentions are very simple to set. They can make a huge difference between a successful interaction and an unsuccessful interaction. Most leaders have intentions for almost every interaction they have. Successful women, specifically, tend to have an intention about each interaction. Here are a few examples:

Prospective client interaction
The intention might be to **be curious** and find out if we have a fit.

Employee interaction
The intention might be **to inspire, motivate, and empower** to lead.

Current unhappy client
The intention might be **to listen** to his or her concerns and find ways to help.

Current happy client
The intention might be **to hear** how our service is helping and continue to support.

Our children
The intention might be **to connect** and let them know we care.

Our spouses
The intention might be **to connect** and let them know we are on the same team.

Why bother setting intentions? In greatly adverse situations, it is critical to have an intention. It keeps us on track. A few minutes into the conversation, ask yourself, "Am I getting what I intended?" If not, stop, take a deep breath, and take charge of the conversation with a powerful energy reset question that will be sure to be seen as a reset.

Setting an intention is not always about meeting your own needs; it may often be about identifying the needs of a group and making sure those needs are met. To clarify, I am not advocating ego-based intentions but rather intentions for the greater good. An ego-based intention would exclusively be about one person's needs without taking into consideration the others in the group.

If your intention is peace, this is only for the greater good of everyone. If an intention is to get back at someone or something, this intention is only ego serving. There is no win-win in such an intention. Pay attention to your own intentions and be sure that they are for the greater good or a win-win situation. Another intention may be to create fun and joy in the day, and who doesn't want that? If, however, your intention is to be heard but not to hear, that too is for your ego's good, but most likely will not lead to greater good. Be sure your intention serves all in the group!

If you set annual goals, try setting intentions to go along with those goals. (If you do not, I hope you will after reading this book.) What you'll find is that intentions both keep you on track and keep you focused on the result you are aiming for. Intentions act like bookends for your goals.

Intentions may also act like bookends for a conversation. If you stay committed to your intention, you step into a more powerful way of being in the world. You tend not to let life drag you around, but instead you tend to be a powerful leader.

This is twenty-first-century leadership!!

My daughter loves riding horses. When she was learning to canter on a horse, she had a lesson in which the horse bucked about two inches off the ground. My daughter was afraid to ride at her next lesson. We discussed her intention for the lesson. She said it was to "stay in charge." I asked what exactly that meant. She was able to describe four things she needed to do: hold shoulders back, heels down, hands still, and stay in strong energy. She got it! She cantered with great success! Now she has this life lesson to look back on. Intentions matter.

INTUITION

The other business tool we have tended not to think about in business until now is intuition. While I believe that we are all using it—men and women alike—women are often less afraid to say that they use their intuition at work. As a matter of fact, they say it with confidence and pride.

One of the exceptions to this, however, includes my friend, Riz Virk, a businessman who has created amazing success in business many times over. He is the successful author of a book called *Zen Entrepreneurship*. He is young, consistent, compassionate, and very aware. After graduating from MIT and spending years of growing and selling successful businesses, he decided to put himself through Stanford University's Graduate School of Business.

Riz recently shared a story with a group of my clients about a conversation he had with people in a master's-level class he was taking. The topic was how to make business decisions. As they spoke about testing, measuring, and researching, he pushed them to better understand the methodology behind the work. He said, "After doing the testing, measuring, and researching, when it comes down to a final decision, there is a moment when you ask yourself, how do I really take the plunge and go for it?" He continued, "When these businesspeople finally got down to it, the answer was: 'Listen to my gut!'" You see, thanks to Riz, even at Stanford they are talking about the power of our intuition when it comes to business.

Women use this skill almost without thinking about it. Therefore, wildly successful women tend to be quick on their feet. They make decisions quickly because there is less weighing of options over and over. They are able to be quiet enough to hear their intuition's whispers and are confident enough to listen to them.

So let's back up just for a moment to be sure we are all on the same page. Intuition has been defined as "immediate cognition without the use of conscious or rational processes," as well as "a perspective insight gained by the use of this faculty."

This has been described for years as our sixth sense. Women are amazing at using their intuition. As the number of women business owners has continued to grow over the past 25 years, it is not surprising to find that they are using their intuition in business, as well as in every other aspect of their lives.

Wildly successful women use their intuition every day, all day, and because of it are extremely efficient and effective in their decision-making. This is not to say that men do not; Riz is a great example of a man who has used his intuition extremely well over the years. But women seem to rely more heavily on their intuition at work and in business—and it serves them well.

Here are two great quotes that speak to this topic from both the male and female perspective:

"When I see danger, I step away. When I think I can move forward, I move ahead, and when I think I can come closer, I do. Sometimes I am wrong, but often, if I pay attention, I am right, and these maps of my own instincts guide me as surely as any by Rand McNally would."—Mary Morris

"Every time I've done something that doesn't feel right, it's ended up not being right."—Mario Cuomo

So how do we develop this skill? First and foremost, let's break down the steps to using intuition.

Step #1: Notice your intuition. We need to be aware enough that we know we have intuition about something, and quiet enough to listen to it. Start to notice that you have many choices and how various choices feel inside your body. Play around with the various choices. Choose one and stand in that choice to see how it feels. Choose another. Stand in that choice and notice how that choice feels. So first, we must notice our intuition.

Step #2: Acknowledge it. We need to be aware enough to know to stop and hear the voice of our intuition and to acknowledge it. Noticing that we have this voice within us is critical, but sometimes we move so fast we do not even notice it. Slow down and notice that there are feelings around choices. Stop and acknowledge the voice of intuition. Know that there is not just the reasonable and rational voice but also the wise voice that desires to be heard. First notice it and then acknowledge it! Notice whether or not you are listening to it with validity.

Step #3: Trust your intuition. Trust yourself enough to take the action (or no action) on the issue or decision. This is probably the most difficult step. Trust yourself and act. Dive in. Notice. Acknowledge. Trust.

I speak to so many women who get hung up on step #1. Their intuition is speaking to them about something, but they are ignoring it. They weigh a decision over and over and over again, wasting endless energy, time, and resources. When we notice that we are spending lots of time and energy "thinking" about a decision, it is a great indicator that we are ignoring our intuition, and if we were to follow the three easy steps outlined above, we could have made a decision effectively and efficiently that would allow us to keep moving.

Another thing we often have a tendency to do is to act slowly rather than just listening to our intuition and acting when we really already know, especially if we think a certain decision should take a certain amount of time. For example, if we know what we want in a house and the first house we look at has every single feature that we have on our list, we tend to think we need to look at more—"just because." Our rational brain is saying, "This is one of the biggest purchases in my life. I want to be sure it is perfect." But how many times do we end up back at the first choice?

Bottom line, intuition is a business tool of the twenty-first century and serves us amazingly well, should we choose to use it!

WHAT IS SUCCESS?

I end with this because this is always an interesting conversation. So many define success as being able to retire and having X amount of money in the bank. But really, success has nothing to do with that. To me, success is you living your extraordinary life and impacting the world the way *you* want to. That is success, and we don't need to do that in 10 years, 20 years, or 50 years; we get to do that *today*. When we start to focus on our *intentions*, we realize this. The goals are important, but how we are choosing to be each day is even more important, and when we work at who we are being today—we have huge impact.

To me, success is not success without looking at the big picture. For example, no amount of money in the world would be payment enough for me to not spend quality evenings with my daughter. No money in the world would be payment enough to not allow me to set my own calendar. But to others, that may not be the case.

CREATING A FULL, BALANCED LIFE

I have heard it hundreds of times from women in all kinds of businesses: "I am afraid of success, because if I get too successful, my family life will suffer." "I will not be able to balance it all." "I won't have the lifestyle that I have now." The truth, however, is to the contrary! In fact, the more successful we are, the more we can have the lifestyle we want!

Having a balanced life is really bogus! There is no such thing as a balanced life. What is balanced to me may not be balanced to you.

I move a mile a minute; it is my New York nature. A balanced life is really about having the space to do all that you want over the course of time.

This may seem like I've made a sharp left turn here, but give me a minute. When my daughter was a baby, between one and two years old, she started to eat less of what I put in front of her and more of what she wanted. If I looked at what she ate for just one day, I would make myself crazy. It did not always seem balanced. But if I looked at what she ate over the course of the week, she ate very well. I had to stop looking at the trees and look at the forest. Having a balanced life is sort of like that.

We have to look at the big picture of our life.

If we go back and look at our goals and our goal wheel or the sections of our lives—health, personal/spiritual growth, career/business, money, significant other, family/friends, recreation, and environment—we cannot do something in every single category every day. On the other hand, if we look at a week, I am confident that we can touch on something in each category.

Creating a life like that is about choice. It is about having that greater vision for your life and beginning to create that today. It is about knowing your priorities. It is about getting clear on what to say no to and what to say yes to. When we say yes to one thing, we are also saying no to many other things. Creating a balanced life is about truly becoming CEO of your life.

As you create your vision, you'll begin to notice that your story has a tone to it. It might include words like relaxed, decadent, warm, friendly, calm, impactful, and healthy. Let's pretend that those words are used to describe your vision. You would want your lifestyle to begin to reflect that tone.

This does not mean you do not work! This means you do your work in a way that has great impact. If you have employees, of course you want to be a role model, but you can also set up the fact that you are the owner and take great pride in being a part of your family's life at certain times. In no uncertain terms do we want others to be a victim of their lives. I think that our current world culture is so victim-focused, we share how much we work, how awful it is, and we almost compete in how stressful our lives are. More work equals "bigger victim." Mistake! The goal here is to design a life that works for you.

When we step out of the victim mentality, we step into our powerful best-self mentality. It is the only place from which we can create the lifestyle that enables us to feel powerful, in charge, and balanced.

I believe we also have made a mistake in assuming that working 40, 50, 60, 70, or 80 hours equals how much money we will make! This is not accurate! There are many of us who work twenty to thirty hours and still make a full-time income! I learned this the hard way. I used to work 80-plus hours a week in my old business. We have to change our paradigms, however, to do so.

The most successful people have found a creative way of working and making their work style work for them. It is not just about hours but about how we choose to spend our hours that helps us attain work-life balance, if there is such a thing.

DOING

What needs to be in place to achieve work-life balance? First and foremost, you need a vision, and the belief that you need to create a style of life that resembles that vision now—not 10 years from now. This balance issue that continues to come up has two parts to it. One is the logistics of being more balanced.

Here are some examples of logistical moves we can make to help us become more balanced:

1. Quality time with family. Choosing to pick up my daughter from school each day is one way I choose to have quality time with her every single day. So, choose quality time with family. It does not have to be long. A few minutes each day is invaluable.

2. Book it! I also put my workout schedule in my calendar on a weekly basis. That schedule is just as important as my work, if not more important! Schedule things that you typically let go by the wayside if you are committed to impact your life here.

3. Daily goal review. Look at your goals on a regular basis and be sure that, within your week, you create the time and space for each area of your life.

4. Three goals per day. Set only three goals each day taken from your goal sheet or to-do list—no more. Meet your commitments to yourself (more on this later in the book). Accomplish those things early in the day and then allow the rest of your day to unfold naturally.

5. Keep it simple! People think that in order to have more fun and recreation, it means more vacations! Crazy! What could you do every day for five minutes that is pure joy and fun for you? It might be to walk outside and notice the flowers, stop and really listen to the birds, or bring a massage therapist into the office every Friday for everyone who wants to partake. Bring fun and joy into every day, rather than put it off for the next vacation! Bring a tiny bit of the feeling of vacation into your world today. It changes the feeling of the day.

6. Acknowledge. Take two minutes out of each day to acknowledge someone, either at home, at the office, or both. Doing this makes us switch our energy to what we are truly happy about rather than things that frustrate us. Acknowledge those around you; it changes the tone of the day!

7. Bold actions. Take a bold action every day toward a big goal. Progress makes us feel productive. It makes us feel that we are in a state of action and that we are in charge of our world. Bold actions are key to balance. Take a bold action in each area of your life on a regular basis.

8. Health and fitness. Years ago, I was in the fitness industry. We (mistakenly) make people feel like workouts need to be an hour to an hour and a half long. This is not really necessary for basic good health. Dr. Mehmet Oz, cardiac surgeon and co-author of *YOU: The Owner's Manual* and *YOU: On a Diet* (among others), debunks some of the ideas we used to have about fitness, including:

> Increase your heart rate only 60 minutes per week! We need this for peace of mind anyway. That can translate to taking three 20-minute power walks a week. Take a break to do this during work hours if you can. You need it!

> Walk 10,000 steps daily. (Wear a pedometer to see if you are close!) Park a few rows out in all parking lots. Take the stairs, not the elevator, and you'll quickly make headway toward reaching 10,000 steps.

> Work in only five minutes a day of stretch/flexibility exercises! It makes a difference!

> Incorporate strength training into your workout schedule. 15–20 minutes a few times a week can make a big difference!

Practice mindful moments throughout the day. What could this look like? Breathing conscious at red lights, eating all meals at a table, and focusing on eating. Having an eye-to-eye conversation. Taking time to deep breathe before or after meetings, just to name a few.

9. Simplify! Throw things away. Be clutter-free. Messiness and accumulating stuff creates negative energy that truly leaves us feeling more heavy, more unbalanced, and adds to our to-do list. I am a huge believer in creating clutter-free space!

10. Stop multitasking! Yes. Stop! We think that this allows us to get more done. But really, it makes us crazy! Do one thing at a time and do it well. Let's get more mindful about whatever the task is at hand. Love the task at hand.

11. Color Code! I like to use three colors in my to-do list as well as my calendar. The three areas are family, work, and me. Color-code these in your calendar, and you will see if you are creating a balanced life.

When we multitask, we do not fully enjoy anything we are doing.

We can do this! Once we start to integrate these logistical things into our daily routines and burst out of our boxed-in way of thinking, we quickly begin to experience a sense of freedom.

I think it is important that we know some of the facts of today's world, not to think of ourselves as victims but to understand why our fast pace exists. In doing so, we can be more conscious and deliberate about managing our lives in a more balanced way.

The amount of information we receive today in one day is equal to what our grandparents received over the course of their lifetime. According to 2004 U.S. Census figures, 67 percent of working-age couples are dual income, and that percentage has, no doubt, gone up since then. Both parents choose to work to support the lifestyle they want. When one person is not dedicated to the functioning of the household, there is more for all members of the household to do.

During the past 25 years, women's roles have drastically changed. Someone I know shared a story about her boss's response when she told him she was pregnant. "We are sure going to miss you," he said, assuming she was going to stay home with her new baby. In our twenty-first-century world, we would never think of saying such a thing, because we know that a woman can absolutely have a career or business and also be a mom.

However, women are making conscious choices so that we can do it all. Many are choosing to have fewer children; others are waiting until later in life to begin a family. Still others are finding creative ways to combine work and family through operation of a home-based business, or negotiation of flexible hours at their workplace.

Women are choosing to have a life where they can contribute to their family's income, their family's household, and the needs of the world. I believe this is as much out of choice as it is how the world is evolving. Women see themselves as having value for contributing in all areas. This is global progress! Michael Gerber, author of *The E-Myth Revisited*, says it well: "The difference between great people and everyone else is that great people create their lives actively, while everyone else is created by their lives, passively waiting to see where life takes them next. The difference between the two is the difference between living fully and just existing."

Women are choosing to do it all but, at the same time, are not becoming victims to the lifestyle that comes with it. We can do it all in a crazy and unbalanced sort of way (which is not really success, in my opinion) or we can find our unique ways of not following all the "rules of the world" in order to do it all. This allows us to be more powerful as individuals too. It allows us to be unique in our thinking so that when something is not working, we can stop and think about a new approach to that situation. I believe that women see that we are in this world to contribute in a way that is unique to them, that is productive, and that adds value to the world.

"I am here to live out loud."—Emile Zola

I believe we are all seeking our individual paths to "living out loud!" There is truly no other way, is there?

So many people complain to me that their to-do list is so long! They go on and on about how much they have to do, and my response is always, "Congratulations, you are alive!"

As long as we are alive we will probably have some sort of to-do list. It is, however, our choice to decide our relationship with it. Does it run you or do you run it? What is *your* relationship with your to-do list? Do you let it overwhelm you or do you see it as your vision in action?

I try to get very conscious about my to-do list, only putting things on it that are aligned with my vision. In doing so, I find myself getting excited about all that is on it. I know that I cannot and do not have to do it all today. It is there just to remind me of things that I want to accomplish as I am on this journey to "the vision." Don't get me wrong! I prioritize, yet usually accomplish less than what I set out to do in a given time. At the same time, I try to allow my to-do list to be just that—my guide for the day or the moment—and enjoy the task I said yes to that is currently at hand. Would I rather be bored? I cannot think of a time in my life when I was ever bored! There is always something to do, to be, to create, or to learn. There are always thoughts and ideas to entertain.

"I never allow myself to be bored, because boredom is aging.
If you live in the past you grow old, and dull, and dusty."
—Marie Tempest

So, again I ask, "What is this thing called work-life balance anyway?" I believe the entire paradox of this issue is this: Slow down, be in the moment, and love what you are doing in this moment. Know that you have a list a mile long of other fun, great projects on your plate and, if you have things on your list that you do not want to do, give them to someone else who loves them! Live fully, right now, in this moment! Smile. Be happy. All we have is this moment. We keep talking about work-life balance, but bottom line, it is about doing a little bit regularly in all aspects of our lives consistently.

Consistency is really the only thing that has great impact on work-life balance. Taking care of ourselves consistently has us feel as though we do take care of ourselves.

Abraham Lincoln reportedly said, "In the end, it's not the years in your life that count. It's the life in your years." We want to be sure that, every day, we have life in our days! After all, if we don't, we go to bed at night wondering when life is going to start.

BEING

We have discussed the doing aspect of the work-life balance formula—things we can do differently. But I would be remiss if I neglected the other side of this issue. That includes the being, how we need to be in order to achieve balance. Here again, a paradox exists. We cannot achieve balance. We are living, breathing beings, and if we try to achieve balance without being balanced, we will never achieve it. So the being portion of this formula is truly the secret to work-life balance. If we were in a yoga class but we constantly just did the movements or completed the poses without feeling or being more relaxed, we would not truly be doing yoga. It's the same with work-life balance.

It is a state of being!

What does that state of being look like? Here are some suggestions:

1. Breathe. Really breathe, deep down to your toes. Fill your entire chest cavity. If you actually put one hand on your chest and one on your belly, both hands should move if you are truly breathing.

2. Slow down. I find this one challenging, but when I get conscious enough to be aware of the silly speed at which I am moving, I breathe, slow down, and life magically changes!

3. Notice your surroundings. When I do the first two steps, I realize, "Ah, the wind is blowing, the chimes are singing, the water on the lake is calm, the sun is out, and the air is warmer." When we do this, we begin to engage all our senses and, in doing so, life is more balanced.

4. Acknowledge each other. This was also part of the doing list, so that must mean it is ultraimportant! But acknowledg-

ment is not just something to do; it is a way of being. When we get out of our own way enough to be able to see how others are being and what they are doing, we can acknowledge them. This actually starts with a way of being in order to do it well and consistently.

5. Yes or no? Be clear, conscious, and aware of choice in every single thing you are saying yes and no to. This guarantees that you will enjoy life more. It is when we fill our lives with "shoulds" that we begin to resent the world and ourselves.

6. Be silent. Amid the noisy world find silence. I notice silence at a red light. I notice silence after asking a question. I notice silence in a gaze. I notice silence while waiting for a plane. The world is a very, very noisy place. But if we actually look for the silence, it is everywhere. And in that silence, work-life balance is found.

"Go placidly amid the noise and haste, and remember what peace there may be in silence."—Max Ehrmann, *Desiderata*

---

7. Be in the moment. Moments matter. In work-life balance it is the moments that matter. In our fast-paced days, when we can pause for a moment to acknowledge someone, to smile at someone, to hug someone, it changes the mood of the day. Be present and pause and embrace the current moment with a loving gesture. It's a game changer!

8. Be grateful. As they say, create an attitude of gratitude. I remember that when my daughter was three years old, we began ending our day together asking, "What are you grateful for?" She

was three and she got it! She would tell me two things she was grateful for, and I shared mine with her. We have continued to do that, and it is a fun way to spend time at the end of the day. For an entire month, she told me she was grateful for "the puppy that JoJo gave me." Other days, she says, "I'm grateful for you, Mommy," and she gets to hear that I am grateful for her. She hears that I am grateful for others—for things we do, things we have, and experiences we create. I also tell her things I am grateful for about my work. I tell my colleagues in conversation what I am grateful for rather than finding something to complain about. It is amazing how quickly it changes the tone of the conversation! Try it!

9. Be joyful about the little things. We tend to skip over them, but stop and be joyful about things that you are truly joyful about. Celebrate in that moment. This is much like gratitude, but slightly different. It is about bringing joy back into your life consistently. I notice how many people don't laugh anymore, and when something is funny, we chuckle. Live out loud and laugh out loud!

10. Reflect. Notice your life. Notice your body. Notice. Notice. Notice. Be curious. It is amazing how much of life we miss and how much you'll see by just reflecting. It is the only way we see our progress, others' progress, and the world's progress. Reflect. Notice. Be curious.

This quote best summarizes my thoughts on work-life balance:

"The foolish man seeks happiness in the distance; the wise grows it under his feet."—James Oppenheim

A FEW OTHER IMPORTANT INSIGHTS

If you take the time to set your goals and intentions for the year, and stay conscious throughout the year, You will be awed by what the universe conjures up for you. I know I am! Sometimes those synchronicities and coincidences leave me speechless. Stuff that I could never make up. And that constantly leaves me in awe of this amazing life.

I love this bumper sticker I've seen: "If you are not in awe, you are not paying attention." And that means you are probably distracted by complaining, blaming, being right, or judging someone being wrong. Don't miss the magic, my friend. Look for the awe, the amazing, whispers, coincidences, and the universe conspiring in your favor.

Ralph Waldo Emerson said: "Once you make a decision, the universe conspires to make it happen." Don't miss that! Sometimes we miss it because we think it should look a certain way, so it passes us by.

Another important practice that I think is critical to success is living your life from a place of gratitude—it is a lens through which we can choose to see our life every day. A habit of gratitude is a transformative tool. To me, gratitude is the doorway to success, whatever success you are looking to create, in any aspect of your life.

The purpose of having your goals written on one piece of paper is to give you focus. You want to keep your eyes on the goals and possibilities, not the obstacles and the fears. You need to be aware of what you see in your mind's eye. Notice what your mind is giving attention to and know that you have a choice about it.

A reminder here: Goals are meant to be aimed for, but are not always meant to be reached. By aiming for them, you accomplish much! In doing so, you make major strides that you can both hang your hat on and learn from in order to keep going. If you think about any big goal that you have accomplished, wasn't it often true that difficulties tended to increase the nearer you approached the goal? When it seems the hardest, keep going!

Reaching goals is not always easy, but striving to reach them is an opportunity for personal growth. Many times I have set goals and not achieved them. However, what I did achieve was gaining some new lessons and knowledge from the experience that makes me wiser, more savvy, and more ready to dive into the next goal. Wise, conscious people always find the silver lining and are grateful for it.

Achieving goals is truly hero's work.

John F. Kennedy said: "As we express our gratitude, we must never forget that the highest appreciation is not to utter words, but to live by them."

Wishing you wild success, happiness, and authentic learning in ALL aspects of your life!

USING YOUR GOAL WHEEL

There are many ways to utilize the goal wheel. I have my goal wheel on a big corkboard with pictures all around it representing my goals. Pictures are worth a thousand words, as you know. So having the picture of what you are "going for" to see each day can be extremely motivating. I *love* looking at it each day, and I ask myself, **Is what I am doing today aligned with my goals?**

The *best* way to use your goal wheel is to look at it regularly and share it with someone who will discuss it with you regularly who you can have an accountability agreement with (like a professional coach). This is the most powerful way to use it. Have a weekly meeting with yourself and the wheel and your to-do system (a masterfully simple and efficient to-do system e-book coming next—stay tuned!), and be sure that what you are setting out to do this week is aligned with that wheel.

Remember, there is magic just in this process, About 25 years ago I took my goals and put them in a book . . . and then closed the book and did not look at it for at least a few years. To my surprise, when I took that book out again and looked at it, I had accomplished many of those goals. For example, on one page, I had put two cars: a BMW convertible and a Jeep Cherokee. To my surprise, those two cars were now parked in my garage!

GOALS AND FAMILIES

Now here is a game changer: Do the wheel with your kids!! Do it as a family! I have one client who does it every year with her four children and husband. They take an hour or so and each go off and do their own personal wheel, and then they come together and share their wheel with everyone. Then they create a *family* wheel—of things they all want to do together. It warms my heart to think how we are changing families when we do this! These are some of my very favorite stories. Please share with me if you choose to do this with your family. Kids love adding pictures to their goals too.

I have been using this tool now since 2002. I have done this process in a retreat format. I have done it over the phone thousands of times one-on-one. I have done it in teleclass format dozens of times. What I have witnessed is that, over time, we change with this process. My ego is less in the goals—it is now more about the integrity of who I choose to be each day and living that vision fully today. This goal wheel helps us to do just that. It is a powerful tool if we choose to use it.

I want to hear from you!! As you do this process, please email me. Let me know your experience with this tool. I also offer a one-time, one-hour coaching session to do this if you want some guidance and support to develop your goal wheel. No charge! What people tell me is that the wheel "speaks to them much better" after our session. I have one client that said, a few months after we completed the wheel together, "Every time I look at the goal wheel, I want to kiss it!" This is exactly how you want to feel when you review it; it should get you excited about your life—right now!

If you enjoy this tool and want more, check out my various programs at www.lorinbeller.com—and join the tribe of like-minded *conscious leaders* in the world.

If you are an entrepreneur and want to step up your business, I have developed a business wheel based on the model. Again, a tool that will have you thinking about your business in a whole new way!

Finally, I have also developed a graduate wheel for those of you who have mastered the first one. It has a game changer component to it. I reserve that for our master-level goal setters. It will support you in stepping up your game, guaranteed!

Every year in early December I offer an annual goal call to walk people through the process of using this tool. Some have done the call every year since 2002!! That is how powerful a tool it is. And it can be done any time of year!

I have seen this tool change lives. I have seen it create focus and clarity. I have seen it increase self-confidence. I have seen it bring families together. I have seen it turn entrepreneurs into leaders. What it always does, if you use it to have a regular meeting with yourself, is get you in *focused action*—that is how life changes.

DON'T DO IT ALONE

The final point is that when we set goals, we often think we need to do it all ourselves. This is especially true of women, but we do not need to do it alone. I love the signs on some of the ski slopes around the country that say, "Do not ski alone!" It is true here, too. Do not try to complete your goal alone! Wildly successful women ask for help! They delegate, they reach out, they identify goals and who might be able to help them; they ask those close to them and they also ask those they may not know but who have blazed the trail ahead of them.

Recently, I met a woman leader who was in the audience during one of my keynote speeches. Afterward, she told me she liked what she heard and said, "If there is any way I can help you, let me know." She offered her card and left it in my court. A few weeks later, I called her to ask if she'd be willing to do an interview for a book I was writing. She was happy to participate, and after the interview she again offered to help. She taught me something about asking for help. Sometimes we ask for help when we are at our lowest, but really, the place to ask for help is when we are doing our best!

So, once you complete the writing of your goals, revisit them through the lens of "who can help me." Begin to make a list of allies you can call upon along your journey. Ask them for help in a very specific way. Most of the time, you will find they want to help and would be happy to do so! Your journey to your vision should not be a lonely one, but one that is filled with an abundance of allies along the way. You'll find that you will, in turn, want to be allies with others on their journey.

"Tell me, what is it you plan to do with your one wild and precious life?"—Mary Oliver

CONCLUSION

Now that you have completed this goal-wheel tool or are committed to doing so, the goal wheel is not about the goals! What does that mean?! Really, the goals are about **informing your journey** *today*. I hope that this goal tool inspires you to live your best life *today*. I love this wheel because it gives us permission to "dance among each day." If we only focus on our work, we leave the other sections out. If we only focus on our health, we leave the other sections out. This tool gives you full permission to live a full and balanced life *today*. I love that! So do your goal wheel and live fully today with that annual intention in mind always!!

ABOUT THE AUTHOR

Lorin Beller has been working with this goal-setting tool both personally and professionally since 2002. Thousands of clients have used it with amazing success. What Lorin has learned is that goals in life are critical to our success, yet how we go about them needs to be aligned with our authentic behavior. And when we align our intentions and behaviors with our actions, that is when magic is created, because the universe conspires with us. Working with hundreds of clients over the years, Lorin has witnessed firsthand the power of this goal-setting tool. It is simple, yet profoundly deep, and changes who we are being in order to accomplish great things while we walk our journeys on this planet. Lorin believes that we each bring a unique and special perspective to life, and when we choose to be fully responsible for our behaviors and impact in the world, we live our purpose each day extraordinarily. Our extraordinary journey does not start when you get "there"; it starts now.

FOR MORE INFORMATION

This tool is impactful all on its own, and some people find that using the tool with a professional coach makes all the difference. Lorin Beller and her team have been providing professional coaching services since 2001. We offer private one-to-one relationships and groups that focus on Entrepreneurial Development as well as Mindful Leadership. We also offer women's retreats in the heart of the Adirondacks on the East Coast in upstate New York, as well as in San Diego on the West Coast. To find out if this team might be who you have been looking for to partner with you on your extraordinary journey, email Lorin for a sample coaching session. This free service is offered as her calendar allows. Email lorinbeller@gmail.com. For more information on the services that Lorin Beller & Co. provide, please go to www.lorinbeller.com

Big Impact

www.ingramcontent.com/pod-product-compliance
Lightning Source LLC
Chambersburg PA
CBHW031730210326
41520CB00042B/1747

* 9 7 8 0 9 7 6 9 5 5 8 3 2 *